SHOOTING ARROWS
AT THE MOON

Poetry and Prose Poems

by

Nancy Wakeman

Meridien PressWorks
San Francisco

2004

Published by:
Meridien PressWorks
J. Powell, Publisher
P O Box 640024
San Francisco, CA 94164
415-928-8904
meridienwriters@aol.com

Printed by: copy.net

ISBN 1-891132-07-5

Cimarron Poetry Series

Jeanne Powell, publisher
Meridien PressWorks
P. O. Box 640024
San Francisco CA 94164
415-928-8904
meridienwriters@aol.com

Chandra Garsson
Insomnia (Awakening)

Kimi Julian
Seventeen Poems and a Fragment

Drea Brown
Just Brown

Christopher Bernard
The Dilettante of Cruelty: Deserts

Craig Easley
Deja Voodoo, The Tongue Never Sleeps, Millennium Man

Tony Sanchez
Just Drunk

Anne Bacon Soule
The Fat Lady Sings

Phillip T. Nails
Sexological Asylum

Nancy Wakeman
Shooting Arrows at the Moon

To Josee Andrei
and
all anonymous artists

Special thanks to Gloria Rodriguez for giving so
much of her time and energy.
To Amy Wilson for her encouragement.
To the WWW group for their support.

CONTENTS

SHOOTING ARROWS AT THE MOON

STAGES OF LIFE

The girl climbs to the crown of the oak tree
and shoots arrows at the moon. Her tiny nipples
swell with excitement. She wants to pull
the moon close to her, to touch it.
Her missiles curve down, silver splinters
shimmering in the earth.
On moonless nights she runs,
howling with the wild dogs.

The moon rises and sets. Rises and sets.
The earth turns.

The woman tucks her lips around her teeth,
tucks blankets around her children,
closes the window to shut out the moon.
Her breasts are full of wine,
she is drunk with love.
No one will steal her children.
Slivers of silver slip into the room,
dusting the broken bow,
filling the empty quiver, kissing
the children. Under the bed a spaniel pants
and suckles her litter.

The moon rises and sets. Rises and sets.
The earth turns.

The crone strings the bow. Slips silver
arrows under her granddaughter's pillow
and flies out the window.
Her breasts hug her body like empty wine skins.
She blesses the dogs, barks at the trees.
When she reaches the rim of the world she jumps

and catches the horn of the new moon.

The moon rises and sets. Rises and sets.
The earth turns.

SHEILA

Sheila, steady in her silent love, flopped her snaky arm around my shoulders, sharing my dreams and secrets. Dressed in Woolworth's best, a green and pink ruffled plaid, her long legs swayed. Her feet, shod in cracked patent leather, danced over the Persian carpet beside my faded sneakers.

Cowboy brother galloped by, lassoed a leg, snatched her from me, dragged her upstairs. I tried to rope and tie him with my screams. Sheila's soft limbs flailed the air. Her head hit every step. Her feet flying, they danced on his bed. Gray stuffing oozed from her ankle. Shrieking, I attacked. Jumped on the bed. Grabbed Sheila's hand, only to slip and fall like a rag doll. My head cracked on the radiator.

Sheila and I screamed through the house. Ran to the safety of the kitchen. Mother dropped the spaghetti dinner when she saw the red river running down my back, They tore Sheila from me. Father wrapped me in a blanket. His huge hands held me still on the Formica table while the doctor sewed my head.

Faithful Sheila sat slumped in a chair shrinking into her blood stained best dress. Plastic forehead fractured, gray brains spilling out. Silent in her suffering. I wanted to sew up her ankle, to stop her dreams from spilling out of her cracked skull, but I couldn't so I crowded the kitchen with my screams.

We reclined on our bed, nursing our wounds. Days galloped by, then years. Sheila lost most of her yellow hair, her skin grew too threadbare to repair. Despite her scars and frailty she became ever more lovable and found many friends.

Now I stand alone, painting my self-portrait. The skull is sliced open, brains made of thick brown paper and shiny string tumble out. My lips are painted white with politeness. I cannot scream.

ENGAGED TO JESUS

I rubbed the white dress and felt the bumps made by the pattern of leaves and flowers.

"A-line style, that suits you," my mother said. The tag said, "size 15– Chubette". I was only thirteen. My mother liked the dress because it covered the rolls and lumps of my flesh. I fingered a veil pinned to the wall behind the dress rack. It was stiff with layers of ruffles.

"I have to have a veil," I said.

"You're not getting married," my mother sighed. "You don't need such an elaborate veil." What she meant was: *all those layers of ruffles will make you look even fatter.*

My eyes misted as I stared at myself in the mirror. How I longed to be a bride of Christ. My great-aunt had married Jesus. Her face was smooth and shiny with joy at every family gathering. Perhaps I was too young, but in two weeks I would be taking my first steps toward the altar. In two weeks I would be confirmed in the Episcopal Church. That was almost like being engaged to Jesus. Jesus was better than James Dean who always had skinny girl friends.

Jesus didn't care what size I was. He didn't tease me and didn't mind that I failed math and French two years in a row. He always welcomed me to church with open arms. He was never angry with me and always knew what to say: "Let not your heart be troubled." or "Ask and it shall be given you; seek, and ye shall find; knock and it shall be opened unto you." Every Sunday light shone through the stained glass figure of Jesus, covered my dimpled hands with rainbow colors, and I was filled with ecstasy.

"You can wear this dress for graduation from grammar school, too." My mother interrupted my day dreaming with her practical words. "Herlihy can make you a veil."

Mrs. Herlihy could do anything – clean, cook, iron and sew. My mother shopped for groceries, played tennis, drove cars and made decisions. But I was the one who decided that I was going to be a Bride of Christ, being confirmed in my white dress and veil was the first step. That meant that I could take Holy Communion and partake of the body and blood of Christ. The Bible said, "Oh taste and see." In two weeks I would taste Jesus' body, drink his blood, swallow his words and be much closer to him.

I didn't care about leaving grammar school and entering junior high. That only meant more problems about trains going thirty miles an hour and the wind blowing eighty miles an hour, and how long does it take the train to get from Detroit to Denver if there is a cow stuck on the track in Des Moines.

I stroked my white dress. Junior high school meant Darwin, evolution and science. I didn't believe in those things. Darwin was a liar. I believed every word in the Bible. God created the heavens, the earth and Jesus. Jesus said, "Blessed are they that mourn for they shall be comforted. Blessed are they which do hunger and thirst after righteousness for they shall be filled."

Jesus was thin and pale, but he was strong. I was big, but weak. Jesus said, "Get thee behind me, Satan!" I gave in to temptation and ate too much chocolate cake, cheated on math tests and stole silver bracelets from Woolworth's. With Jesus I had a chance.

The Sunday after Easter I knelt at the communion rail before the altar. My veil flew around my head like a cloud of white butterflies. Bobby-pins gouged my scalp. In the cup of my hands I held a thin white ghost-like wafer. A little bigger than a quarter. Was this all there was to Jesus?

Father John moved down the rail, wiping the rim of the silver goblet that held Christ's blood with a white handkerchief. I put his thin body into my mouth, grabbed the base of the goblet and tipped it toward my mouth so I could get a big swallow of Christ's blood. His body was stuck to the roof of my mouth. Pink drops of Jesus' sweet blood stained my dress.

I returned to my pew, pretended to pray and dug at Christ's body, still stuck to the roof of my mouth, with my finger. Jesus fed a crowd of five thousand who came to hear him preach with five loaves of bread and two fishes. Why did my confirmation class of twenty get something that tasted like cardboard?

When I walked down the steps of the church Father John chuckled, patted me on the head, welcoming me to the Protestant Episcopal Church. The sleeves of his gown flopped over me like giant moths. My mother clicked her tongue and rubbed the stains on my white dress. I knew she was thinking that I didn't do anything right, but I didn't care. I was engaged to Jesus.

RED BODY

After an empty winter and a hungry spring
she leaves her father's house

Follows the deer trail to the meadow
unbuttons her life and sheds her old skin
Under the red heat of the gold she touches
the red wool coat with the gold buttons
swimming in the shimmering stream

And sees the splashing bear
red eyes buttoned into bristling brown fur
red gummed mouth snapping at insects

She feels the hot blue sky melting into the cold stream
her red soul melting into the blue stream of the sky
And tastes the persistent stained snow melting
under the red blast of the gold sun
buttoned into the blue sky

She hears the hot wooly air bristle
with the scraping sound of insects
buttoned into the humming world

And sees herself buttoned into the red wool coat
buttoned into the brown body of the bristling bear
buttoned into the red body of the humming world

COVERED WAGONS 1957

My hands twisted into fists. I was a prisoner, crammed into our station wagon with my mother, my two sisters, my mother's best friend and her daughter. Our eyes were stained with sleep, our pastel summer clothes stained red from the sleeping bags. Our mouths were sour with dreams interrupted by a midnight thunderstorm at our campground. The air in the closed station wagon was stale with peeled oranges and crackers and peanut butter. My mother had been driving all night. Damp sleeping bags were tied to the roof to flap and dry in the hot wind of dawn.

I was fourteen, too young to drive, too old for the giggling and whining of the younger girls. The station wagon sped through dry, hot land. We were driving west to meet my father who was being a cowboy, complete with Stetson hat and chaps, in the White Mountains of Arizona. My eyes fluttered and I thought of the spacious, cool summer home where we usually went at this time of year.

Suddenly a covered wagon appeared, swaying across the desert. My eyes popped open. Another and another. A whole column of covered wagons pulled by tired horses with big ribs, canvas covers shredded to rags, loaded with people.

"Look! Indians!" I cried. Indians so close I could touch them. I had never seen live Indians before. Most of the Indians on television or in the movies were really white people. When we were younger and ran around in the woods with sticks, I was always the one who pretended to be an Indian. My father had tacked a poster to my bedroom wall showing Indians from different tribes – Ute, Shoshone, Navajo, Apache, Seminole, Sioux – dressed in beaded buckskin or shimmering velvet, hands heavy with turquoise and silver.

My mother had to slow down and stop so the covered wagons could cross the road. These Indians wore faded shirts, dusty jeans and cracked lace-up shoes.

"Let's get out," I said, excited for the first time since we had started our trip. "Where are they going?" I wanted to talk to them, to touch them. Everyone at home was white, went to the same school, the same church, the same country club and wore plaid Bermuda shorts in the summer.

"No," my mother said. "Lock your door. Roll up your window."

"They are going to the Indian Powwow at Flagstaff," said my mother's best friend, Peggy, who read the maps and knew everything.

"Why are the wagons so ragged?" I opened my hand to wave at them. They were full of people – children, grandparents, in between people. I couldn't see any suitcases or bags of food.

"Why aren't they wearing any turquoise or velvet?"

"Because they are poor. I wish they would hurry up." My mother tapped the steering wheel impatiently.

"They sell their jewelry or trade it for supplies," Peggy said.

I rubbed the turquoise ring on my little finger, then rolled down the window and felt my small world crack open. Life was bigger than my family, bigger than Hingham, Massachusetts. What was it like to be poor? What was it like to be an Indian? I twisted in my seat and watched the column of covered wagons disappear into the desert.

II

A STORY OF KISSES

The day I was born
battle ships slid into the ocean
I floated out of a dark dream,
kissing air I lay on my mother's belly,
searching for her nipple.

I kissed sisters and cousins,
teeth sweet with chocolate,
salty necks, sandy hands
as the last days of summer
ran down my legs.

Kissing Emmy-Lou,
mouth full of wonder
what was it like to see
through eyes the color of sky?
Kissing Skippy who smelled
of lead pencils, he ran
when I lifted my skirt.

Jesus promised paradise,
how I longed to kiss
the fingers that placed
the body of Christ on my tongue,
but soon I abandoned Jesus
for the back seats of cars and

marched in Mississippi stepping
over the borders of black and white.
Broke the rules to kiss Earl,
baby – he whispered – baby, baby

13

to the white light that sped
through his veins.

Other names, other lips lost
now I kiss lips that commanded
squadrons of men, lips that tell
the stories of Genesis, the secrets of Zen,
we share a catechism of kisses.

HOW DID MY GRANDMOTHER

On my back   feet in stirrups
ceiling light   harsh and bright
the doctor stubs out his cigarette
          smoke lies over us
he tells me to open my legs
pushes long metal pincers
          up into my vagina
                    I am going to die
               anesthesia doesn't dull the pain
                    I am going to die   the nurse
more distant than the moon
          takes my hand

Before this a voice on the telephone
take the six o'clock bus
stand under the clock in the Baltimore
bus station   carry a copy of TIME
I will find you

Before that I lay on a leather couch
no one on top of me this time only
the smoke from the shrink's Freudian pipe
time ticking   shrinking my savings
to get the name of the doctor
who will uproot this weed
growing in me

How did my grandmother
the one I never knew
live with my mother growing

15

inside of her
did she die in childbirth
did she die when the child
was taken from her and given to strangers

Before that Sunday evenings
with laughter and jazz and rum
on the stained couch
of the chauffeur from Barbados
I celebrated freedom from New England
this doesn't happen to me   he said

And before that
there was the social worker from Queens
both college graduates
I was ready to graduate into life
to know with my body
what I had read with my eyes
him and his white bed and wet belly
and his virgin penis
sliding into my immaculate womb
the sweet surprise of the first time

SEASONS

That summer the sun rained down
burned us red as lobsters
We loped along the beach
foraged for blackberries
with grizzly bears.
And banished fear daring
each other to boldly go
where no man or woman
had gone before.
We dove deep
way beyond the barnacled rocks
swam through the eye of the lobster
trailed does through the state park
and rubbed foreheads with fawns.
I spread my petals pinker
more pungent than a prize peony
smoother than sea kelp
our laughter shook the sun
"Where are your badges?" the ranger said
sniffing the air. "You are trespassing."
"What badges?" we said. "We don't need
no stinkin' badges."

The season changed before our eyes
the sun shrank smaller than a nickel
grizzlies began their migration into sleep
blackberries shriveled, deer disappeared.
In the city towers toppled like toys
hard rains pounded the ground
carnivorous men (yes, mostly men)

17

marched in ancient ruts
rattled the bones of war.
And we remembering
        the blushing sun
                the priceless peony
                        the deep dream of the lobster
opened our eyes to our brothers and sisters.

THE OTHER WOMAN

You were haunted by the ghost of your dead mother and spent months wandering the twisting streets of the strange city. I was haunted by the laughing child in you and took you home with me. You jumped in and out of my bed like a mountain goat, only to return to your closet to sleep with your back pack stuffed with state of the art camping equipment. Your laughter echoed in my mind and stirred the passion in me.

I took you out of the city, into the country and introduced you to her, thinking – he will love me more for doing this. When we set our feet on the trail leading to her you came alive. You bounded up the rocky path. I followed, loving your long legs covered with finely spun gold, loving your gentle calf muscles that rippled with each step you took. You stopped at the top of the trail and turned your pink cheeks and bright smile to me. I thought I was the one you desired. I thought I was the one who made you blush and tremble. I thought....

Now I know it was her with her golden hair, her rolling thighs, her breasts heavy with sweet blackberry nipples ripening in the sun. In your honor she spread out her best carpet of forget-me-nots, in your honor her pine trees sprouted tender green shoots, in your honor she sent a white stag bounding through the woods to greet us.

You walked among all this life with laughter on your lips and the ghost of your mother in your heart. Ignoring the beauty bursting around you, you collected twigs covered with lichens and fungus, hiding them in your backpack to take home and examine to search for clues that would explain the mystery of death.

I was so in love with your laughter that I ignored the shadows hiding in your eyes. We ran down her hills tripping and rolling over each other. I opened myself to you; you crawled inside me looking for hidden treasure. We exploded in a rainbow of light. When we fell apart I saw, not the pink trails of my fingernails meandering down your back, but the delicate tracings of grass and leaves engraved on your flesh.

I knew I had lost you. It was not me you were loving but her. It was not my warm honey you drank but her cold, sparkling stream.

Now I sit in the city, pounding my passion into my typewriter and listening to the mechanical voice on your answering machine, "...gone to the hills of Pt. Reyes...Pt. Reyes...Pt. Reyes."

Oh, my lost love, she has seduced you. Go to her. Run your fingers through her hair. Breathe her pine and eucalyptus perfume. Eat her blackberries. She will rock you in her endless ocean and cradle you between her hills. But walk lightly on her flesh for this is the place where she honors the dead, sending them back to the ocean to be purified for the journey into the next life.

III

COMPOST

the woman digs
in the earth
dirt presses
into the whorls
of her fingers
plants itself
between nail
and tender skin

strands of hair
potato peelings
tea leaves
brittle pages torn
from the book of
common prayer

all decay in
the dark dirt
grow into wild lilies
spring wine
a child with dirty hands

ADVICE

out of the inner
bitch of my heart
comes a sentence
of indeterminate
length advising
a path to follow

the middle way
the buddhists say
through a marsh
bordered with nests
white egrets still
as a lover's kiss
the sun hugging
a wayward sky

CHASING SPIRITS

We sail through blue waves of desert mountains. My mother says she wants to escape the treacherous ice of New England, the northeast wind that blows through her bones.

"Turn left here," I lift my finger, trying to be a good navigator.
"Don't point. It confuses me," she says, claiming the wheel as she claimed the tiller of the sailboat on those summer weekends; while my father − wearing only shorts and sneakers, smelling of salt and sweat − stormed through the cockpit, hands busy with sails and ropes.

Before he died my father traded hoisting sails and pulling up anchors for luxury cattle drives, complete with cocktails and catered barbeques, through the high desert of Arizona, land of his ancestors. My mother stayed home, watched the moon rise, planted sunflowers and tomatoes − pausing to predict shifts in the wind, changes in the weather.

Now we pursue him through a land that confuses her. She is surrounded by mountains − no sea, no salt smalls to guide her. The distant sun wanders through thin clouds.

We stop to paint red buttes, a sky bigger than the ocean. And this woman, who has always believed in long sleeves, pulls off her shirt, rolls up her pants.

"I want to feel the sun on my bones," she says, staring into the heat, paint brush in hand, waiting for my father's hand on her shoulder.

RAMADAN IN YOGYAKARTA

We travel in a foreign land.
She complains of the scarcity
of corn flakes, I lament lost luggage.
She adores Prambanan and marvels
at temples with bare breasted goddesses.
I want enlightenment and pull her up
the steep bumpy steps of Borobodur.
Panting and sweating we reach the top
to find headless buddhas, stone stupas,
the distant volcano that buried
this temple in ash for hundreds of years.

Feet aching, heads throbbing,
we take refuge on the seventh floor
of our cinder block hotel.
The sultry night baffles our Yankee
blood and steals our sleep.
Seeking freedom from steamy sheets
we pad onto the balcony to stand
in thick blackness, waiting for
Easter to dawn. I take her arm
marveling at the fragile flesh,
the tender bones of this woman
who gave birth to me.

Suddenly an orange splinter of light slides
between tree tops and the exhausted night.
Smoke from cooking fires ascends, cocks crow,
Muslim chants weave through the city.
The shell of night cracks open and we
witness the meeting of heaven and earth.

HER "I-TALIAN" GARDEN

She stands in the garden, feet sunk into damp dirt
nourished with dead leaves, potato peelings, egg shells
skin loose as the frayed bathing suit
she has worn for so many years.
She deadheads purple petunias, orange roses, marigolds
and grunting stoops to pick radishes, tomatoes
bright and hot as the muscle of the day
beating down turning her brown as the earth.

Her garden, a riot of color and smell,
is too noisy for the garden club ladies
who dress in pale linen and prefer
neatly made beds with petals of pastel
pink and periwinkle blue.
They gossip about Frannie
and her "I-talian garden".
She waters the zinnias trying
to recall the names of those women,
the ones who label each flower.

The back door slams — children, grand, great
and small clatter down the steps
rushing to catch the biggest wave
boisterous bodies plunging
into the promise of summer
Frannie smiles, shakes her head

Once she raced sailboats and cars
applied paint and perfume to catch fast men.
Now she digs compost into her garden
sinking deeper into the ground with each shovelful,

and remembers old friends – this one deaf,
another blind, that one dead.

IV

FAITH

Fresh peas are essential
garlic is slow growing
Wimps are those guys
who believe that calzone
is on the menu everyday
They are big eaters and play
out the charade of equality
But we are under thy patronage
holy mother and invoke the mystery

Wimps are those guys
who believe that calzone
is on the café menu
They move anyone without
allowing themselves to be moved
We are under thy patronage
dear mother and invoke the mystery
Naturally there are times when we think
you're too pushy and demanding

My friends move everyone without
allowing themselves to be moved
Serve ravioli with lobster sauce
in spite of deep faith in garlic and peas
Naturally there are times when they're
too demanding and pushy
But what does inner life matter
when you can make johnnycake like mom

Or serve ravioli with garlic and peas
in spite of deep faith in lobster sauce
Laughter is the child of a long
friendship with food and fire
What does johnnycake matter when
you have an inner life like mother
Who teaches a popular course
full of biblical quotations

To all those big eaters who
pretend to believe in equality
and know that fresh peas are
essential and garlic is slow growing

BIG EARTH BREATHING

Sun polishes the heaving sea
air sparkles with salt spray
wild mustard explodes
in yellow clouds between rows
of gray-green artichokes
the scent of cow dung rises
from the ground

We roll over the steady road dug
into the skin of the heaving earth
one in a column of mechanical
covered wagons following yellow lines
seeking sun and heat after a dank winter
the roar of tires silences the thudding sea

A straw hatted farmer walks
through steaming fields hoe in hand
my pounding heart pushes
spring blood through my veins
I squirm trapped in this metal box

Your hand crawls
under my skirt
travels up my thigh
seeking my tumescent lips
my soul slips through
a crack in the window
flies into the savage mustard
sinks into fresh soil

You caress only the husk
of myself as we follow

the line of cars driving north
and the big earth
heaves and breathes

SPRING CLEANING

outside a red-headed humming bird smaller than
your thumbs pressing the corners of my mouth
purring kisses hover over my lips
hearts flutter faster than whirring wings

your thumbs press the corners of my mouth
our hearts, hollow as church bells, crack
and flutter faster than whirring wings
sunlight rains through giant clouds

our hearts, hollow as school bells, crack
plum blossoms fall, swirl into gutter
sunlight rains down through fat clouds
young mothers slough off their winter wombs

plum blossoms gone, washed into gutter
rain pays no attention to holy days
weary mothers slough off their winter wombs
I stand in the kitchen scrambling eggs

purring kisses hover over my lips
red-headed humming birds
smaller than your thumbs

CORNBREAD

I stand here in the kitchen cooking,
remember you most gracious Virgin Mary,
and pour all natural corn bread mix into a bowl.
Never was it known that anyone who added
two eggs and one cup milk to the dry ingredients
ever fled to your protection or sought your help.

I pour all natural corn bread mix into a bowl
and remember that anyone who fled
to your protection added two eggs
and almost two cups low fat milk
to the dry ingredients.
Inspired by this confidence, I fly
to your protection, implore your help
and seek your intercession.

For fun I add one-half cup grated cheese
a handful of green chiles and canned corn.
Inspired by this sudden confidence I fly
to stand before you covered with flour,
coated with one-half cup grated cheese
and a handful of green chiles.

Oh mother of the word baking
in this golden corn bread,
mother of me covered with cornmeal,
spattered with ignorance
despise not my mixed up prayers,
but with your gourmet grace
taste their homemade goodness.

HANDS

My father sat next to me that summer evening
his huge hairy hands – paws, he called them – resting
on his bony knees. I could see the tendons pull
the fingers, curl them into a cup.
His passionate heart closing his hand into a fist,
short black hairs on each finger joint,
longer black hairs on the backs of his hands.

Hands curled around the mast, hands wrestling
the jib into the cockpit, and the wind ruffling
the black hairs on his hands.
Even then his life was a clenched fist,
ideas held in an iron grip,
opinions pounded into the air.
His hand on my elbow at the dinner table,
pushing it into my ribs to teach me
good manners.

Capable hands polishing my school shoes,
fierce hands that welded my fearful hand
to the gear shift as the car bucked and stalled.
Patient hands guiding my stumbling feet
around the dance floor.
Stubborn hands that tried to push my life
into a neat paid-for box.

The fist squeezed his heart tighter
and tighter until angry blood sped
to his brain and he was tied to a hospital
bed, half-blind, speechless, hands tied

to the metal frame with strips of white sheeting,
life still pulsed in him and he looked
up at my mother.

Her life becoming an open hand as his closed
into a fist covered with black hair,
and he looked up at her from white pillows,
tied to his hospital bed, looking for answers.
Do I die now? His life curled into a fist
and death crawling up through his legs.

But on that summer night he wrapped
his huge hairy paw around my hand
and my life stopped spinning.

SINGING FOR PEACE

The train screeches, rocks on its tracks. I sit knee to knee with a modern Madam Defarge who knits peppermint green wool – a belt, a border for an afghan?

We speed through a tunnel under the Bay. Shooting from the best of times for some – fast money, five star Beaujolais flowing from fountains, houses with a room for every week of the year – speeding into the worst of times. The government pounds drums of fear, tells us we have to invade Iraq, depose Saddam Hussein who hides "weapons of mass destruction," while Oakland claims the highest homicide rate in the country and children in Michigan and Colorado carry guns to school and kill their classmates.

In the dark tunnel the window becomes a mirror reflecting the crowded subway car. We all sit with eyes lowered, reading, knitting, dozing. To look directly at someone is to invade that person's space, to invite unwanted glances. Our brave president chomps at the bit of democracy, ready to invade another country to avenge the threats on his daddy's life, to insure a steady supply of oil for our giant cars.

I am on my way to El Cerrito del Norte BART station to join others and sing for peace. The train surfaces in Oakland, speeds above parking lots full of cranes, truck trailers. The five o'clock sky is still blue above San Francisco and so vast that Twin Peaks and the Transamerica Pyramid become tiny silhouettes as the sun sinks behind gray clouds. Even the Bay shrinks under the expanse of sky.

43

The train speeds on through Berkeley. Madame
Defarge keeps knitting. The sun continues to cast off
stitches that melt into long strands of orange and crim-
son. We rush by houses, small square boxes shoved
together between ocean and hills, freeways and train
tracks. And postage stamp yards fenced with rules and
expectations. Above us the deep vastness of the sky
invites us to stretch the muscle of our imagination.
How small our lives, this devotion to war and us over
them.

The train reaches El Cerrito del Norte and I join the
chorus of women, men and children of all ages to greet
commuters with song – "We Shall Overcome," "This
Land is Your Land". Strangers look each other in the
eye and smile, some give a thumbs up, some stop to
sing for a while. The sky continues adding and drop-
ping colors so glorious we gasp and pause in our
singing to watch strands of peach and magenta melt
into indigo before continuing with "Dona Nobis
Pacem."

ENGAGEMENT

How sweet the sound of the flute   light falling over the
hills   rolling waves that don't break   a wobble in the
sound   a sour note   Sour when I said *I love you*   and
didn't   embarrassed by your black smile   your stum-
bling words   confusing right and left   *Good gosh a'mighty
mama ain't you fine*   me with my big belly   *Are you pregnant
dear*   well meaning women asked   No   Pregnant with
searching   knocking   looking to fill   pop pop up
with my place in the world

The city came at me so fast   scrambling me   be nice
say nothing so someone will love   love my fat   burst-
ing out of that church   bursting out of my family
into all the people of the world   sounds of forgotten
ancestors   Voices of the great oaks   talk about fat
how many meters in girth   growing over the hills   cut
down to build houses for gentry   ships   to carry peo-
ple in trade   Jump up   shake your bones   tap the
ground   the air   remember ancient tongues   shake
Oh baby

Back to your blinding smile   I wanted to be loved
didn't believe a word of what you said   took the ring
they thought I would dance the waltz   walk down the
aisle on the arm of my dad   white gloves   white ruf-
fles   white where I lost that ring   a cheap diamond
solitaire   too big for my finger   throwing snowballs in
the Sierras   that's where it disappeared   in the cold
suburbs   Family armed with white respectability
Stick to your own kind   I let you go to Europe

Following your dream to Afghanistan   those embroi-
dered coats you sent   I went to the airport   boxes col-
lapsing   Smell of goat blood got rid of your seed
made myself bleed   told nobody   no body in my body
Still I lusted swung my hips   fluttered my hands   a
vessel   a handmaiden of god   come here baby   let
moma take your cock   that bitter seed   spilling on
the ground   oh daddy   let me eat you   make my own
cock   my own jazz   shuffling down this corridor
crazy days   bang my head to the rhythm   Where are
you now   you drove a tractor   Bought a house in the
suburbs   that smile   con your way from office boy to
rising executive and I

descend   go underground   down to the center of the
earth   the center of myself   ouch   hot in there   too
hot too touch   forbidden flowers   glory in breasts
delight in buttocks   Clap hands   oh soul   clap hands
sing   sing on those slave ships sailing   and to what am
I a slave

the frown passed down   from generation to genera-
tion   surely the sins of the fathers and mothers   go
down from parent to child until we say   Stop

THIEVES LIKE US

"Billy Waterway's godmother," the man said, "remember me?"

My pen stops. Once my claim to fame, I have not heard that name for twenty years or more. Dennis shoots me a smile. Still the same electric energy despite glasses and hair white as the clouds outside the café. Years ago I followed Rainbow, Billy Waterway's mother, to his Big Top Supermarket – bins of Panama Red, Acapulco Gold, Maui Wowee lined up in the living room – a life lived in public. I kept up with his career from drug dealer, to jailbird, to city council member, to medical marijuana farmer.

"Have you heard about the boy?"
"No contact for years...." my tongue stalls, that story too long to tell in one afternoon.
"Our boy is away. Sitting in San Quentin. Busted for armed robbery. Thirty-five when he gets out. Stupid," Dennis says, walking to the door. "Such a waste."

This time my brain hits the floor. That perfect baby buddha who slid from Rainbow's womb into my arms, that child, brighter than the sun who called me "Mom," I almost stole him from Rainbow. He grew tough as nails, bright as a diamond, with his mother's quick tongue. At six he could recite ten thousand reasons why his lemonade was the best.

We were all scheming how to screw the system, make money without working. Rainbow, big and blond, mind quicker than a calculator, who could change points and plugs just like one of the boys, used the stars and planets for family planning and got the state to support her. I began a brief career of petty thievery, stealing *CRIME AND PUNISHMENT, THE LEFT HAND OF DARKNESS, THE DIARIES OF ANAIS NIN* to feed my mind; lamb chops and sea food to stretch food stamps until a grocery clerk spied my game and pursued me up and down aisles singing, "Such a shame. A life ruined for a can of tuna fish on sale." We were such ardent outlaws, practicing free love, free sex; but held prisoner by jealousy, venereal disease, the poverty of our dreams.

We had such big hopes for Billy – mathematical genius, president. He was the one who could steal fire from the gods and survive. From the beginning he surprised us by arriving a few days early. He celebrated his twelfth birthday by stealing a fifth of tequila from the corner store. At fourteen he borrowed his grandfather's car and drove from San Diego to Reno. The follies of an energetic youth living in a dull world, I thought, he will grow. Then his mother borrowed money, disappeared, left me with pocketful of bills. No news for years. Now he sits in prison. I sit in this café stealing words.

C o r s i c a n   W i t c h
(For Josee)

1.

What is found here
        among the oxalis
             and dandelions
                     roots clotted with dirt

I kneel before
        an altar of weeds
             knees bruised
                 from so much praying
for a word   an image   a sign
something
        to fill this big emptiness
             that grows around me

        what you took when you left
             cradled in a swelling taurus moon

I squat   buttocks bobbing
             in the wild daffodils
arm swings
chop dig grunt dig chop
a ferocious gardener   teetering
                     on the edge

is that you
           your fierce will
                     pulling down
clinging to life

as I try to uproot it

2.

Born blind   the old ones on that Mediterranean
island tried to drown you but you grabbed the hand
of life   swallowed the sun   splashed through mud
puddles   stormed barricades on the streets of Paris

translator   teacher   gestalt therapist
a hunger to see the whole picture
poet   painter   tarot-card-reader
sculptor   mother

how you loved the eyes of the world
focused on you
and shone as our
daffodil faces turned
to your light and
followed you
a corsican witch
through the streets
of this polyglot city

3.

We were Shakespeare's daughters
words waited
floating on thick coffee
steaming in our cups

we composed sonnets in praise of the sun
that golden orb
that still hides behind clouds and weeps

My pen slid across the paper   your fingers touched
those raised dots on the metal bar the size of a ruler
you pushed your stylus through thick paper   pop pop
pop   pulled poems smooth as plums from the depths
of your hunger

4.

The great wooden dice
beat on the board
        you bargained
                one more painting   my memoir
                    I have to vote   sing at the hospital

you stormed out
        with lightning and thunder
                hail rattled my windows

now I squat in the dirt
        teetering on the edge
                tugging at this big
                    emptiness you left

A brief biography of the triple goddess

"She who was and is and is forever."

1. golden years

reborn a great pot bellied oak
    sturdier than gertrude stein
        surely shakespeare would have celebrated
            my eighteen foot girth

liverworts lichens and lycopods covered my scars
  bromeliads balanced on my branches
    one or two wayward orchids found a home
    with me and unfurled petals of orange and crimson
        to reveal white clits sleek as snake heads

i achieved the greatest results with simple heinrich
  a refugee from some egyptian campaign
    when he dropped his gun
      I let him fondle my taproot
        and the truffles hiding under my duff
        he trembled and cried
          my sap rose out of season

forget your regiments of tanks
    your life of right-left   right-left
      i snapped   swing
    to the beat of the samba
        every model of a modern
          major-general knows
           the cha-cha

2.

middle age

before that i slipped
        through the suburban turnstyle
                and ate a bushel of garlic a day
                        my children scattered
                                seduced by the glamour of guns
i dressed from head to toe in black
        like the greatest egyptian wife
                pinned orchids of red and orange
                        on my shoulders
studied spanish to water my lips
        collected threads of blood
                poems of pablo neruda
                        pencil on fire i chased
                                words across a burning meadow
until i became
        the simplest lepidopterist
                and produced the greatest results
                        by opening my dress to vast tribes
                                of migrating *mariposas*

3. youth

before that i grew
        green supple as spring
                collected acorn cups and elongated
                        my fingers taking snap shots
                                of closely related species of oak
tripped over square roots
        imagined myself esther williams
                swimming sleek as a seal

                or cleopatra beloved
                        of poets and generals
i dove into my sea of dreams
        and produced the greatest results
                with the butterfly stroke
                        floated through life
in the simplest way
        but my heart hung open
                i swam through back alleys
                        gun pointed at my belly
searching for a god
        who could bleed
                with me every month

author's bio

As a child I could lie in my warm bed and watch the sun and moon rise over the Atlantic Ocean. The full moon left a shimmering path on the water, inviting me to leave the comfort and security of home, to travel and explore new places. I earned degrees in French and Rehabilitation Counseling, worked as a social worker and counselor; followed that mysterious planet west and settled in San Francisco where I have lived for more than thirty years. Now as I sit and write, buns firmly planted in my red chair, I watch the moon rise over the Berkeley hills.

"Shooting Arrows at the Moon" is my metaphor for writing. My words are arrows. Some hit the moon where lunar energy animates them, giving that spark of illumination that makes toes curl and tongues dance. Others fall to earth and become inspiration for more writing.

My other publications include a chapbook and a biography of the golfer, *BABE DIDRIKSON ZAHARIAS: Driven to Win*. My poetry and prose have appeared in *TRICYCLE: The Buddhist Review*, *The Hollins Critic*, *Lynx Eye*, *REED MAGAZINE*, *San Francisco Bay Guardian* and other journals. I read my work in bars, cafes, libraries and other venues throughout the Bay area.

2370 Market St. #374
San Francisco, CA 94114-1575
(415) 437-9753
nancy@delicious13.com